tung

tung

robyn maree pickens

OTAGO UNIVERSITY PRESS
Te Whare Tā o Te Wānanga o Ōtākou

Contents

Keen sight

Brush the bats from your tongue

A skylight is installed

Take care with their furry wing membranes   wrists   thumbs

They have the eyes of seeds

Taste is distributed for oh that hunger leak of honey

Include the humming text

Some months the heaviness reaches my irises. Things that are higher than me like honeybees, skyscrapers, flowering magnolia trees, and jet planes are filled with light and lightness. I know a white-flowering magnolia in a cold part of the country that grows its one flower close to its heart. If heaviness were a place we would lie prone with weights attached to our limbs, phalanges, and pharynx. Each night unseen beings would tune the weights to the right pitch. It can be an uncertain event that shreds the heaviness.

Lover,

I should've hailed you directly as I will be a different person by the time you sense this. How are the dunes, your children, parents, your respiration? I have been just now on the hillside with the tiny red clover mites, the trees opening themselves green and the ocean in the distance. Forgive me if this script sounds affected, I will be reading it aloud to others and this makes me self-conscious and too aware. I am now reading it aloud as if I were writing to you so that the people here do not feel too uncomfortable with the intimacy I express. Perhaps it is already too late for that. Some things we mean to share, other things we don't, and often our bodies betray us regardless.

Lover, how unknowing I am, how little I know. Lover, perhaps I should be wearing a Ramones T-shirt or something hip and ironic because I am neither. I am digressing because if I were to say, large swathes of, coastal areas of, at risk of, prone to, we would be in it, or in it some more and you may feel heavy or heavier. Or if I were to begin by telling you about my recent trip to Mitre 10 and what I bought only to tell you it used to be a tidal flat, a salt marsh, you may feel deceived by anecdote. This tactic wouldn't work with the Forbury Park Raceway as I couldn't fabricate a plausible reason for going there. Unless you dared me and it involved some kind of illicit hook-up. The Raceway used to be a freshwater marsh. Salt water on one side, freshwater on the other. I don't know much about the presence of salt in the meeting of water and land, but I find the relative proximity striking. Someone wrote—a little poetically, a little true—that South Dunedin was built on top of the sea. There is a famous black and white photo taken in April 1923 of a little boy in a rowboat at the flooded southern end of Normanby Street. Most people in South Dunedin do not own the homes they live in. This means that many of the owners have two or more homes but choose not to live in the South Dunedin one. I will reveal myself to be naïve if I say, 'I hope they are not paying too much rent.' No, that would be dishonest, as I know they will be paying too much rent.

The salted and unsalted water that met the land was filled in with sand by pākehā, which I think we can all agree is sadly predictable. The area became prosaically known as The Flat, then later South Dunedin. Lover, I just caught myself person-splaining, do forgive me, although this *is* a monologue. I trust you will help me gently break it up at the end. The Flat is now the single biggest community or communities in Aotearoa threatened with sea-level rise. I have mixed feelings about the words community/communities as they are infrequently applied to wealthy people. And yes, as you often remind me, lover, there are communities or constellations of beings other than humans who will be affected by rises.

Often sea-level rise is described in scientific literature as if the sea just decided to rise and expand of its own accord. It's like when people talk about prison ratios without talking about systemic racism, or civil war and poverty without talking about colonialism and the World Bank. We know it is our actions causing the sea to rise, but we also know that 'we' and 'our' need a whole lot of nuancing and contextualising. Oh, I've done it again, lover, with my splaining … It's the we who use more energy and buy more things than others—typically a we who has taken from other people—who are responsible.

It took me a long time to realise that wealthy people tend to live higher up.

Lover, I took your advice: at the moment I'm only watching shows and films set before the internet because they're peaceful, or peaceful and violent in different ways. In the 1600s a man said, 'And why would you want to mark the hours in a day?' and I was shook, as they say. Perhaps we do because there is a glasshouse in the high sky and there are tipping points to monitor. Years and centimetres and degrees are triangulated. But it is not enough to say the green will storm the earth if we are gone because so many precious ones of all persuasions are lost each day. Not so much lost but losted, like the intentionality of disappeared. Intentionality? Perhaps losted to insufficient collective care. Lover, this is a ramble because it is vast—the connections are vast and too much for individuals to carry alone.

Sometimes I just want to write 'it is vast' without having to think about all the things that are vast, like loneliness or desire, which in turn could be written about differently: the gap in a forked tree instead of loneliness, or a scene involving a wolf for desire perhaps. But these vast interconnections are like the small, embedded word at the beginning of cryosphere. You see why I need that Ramones T-shirt? I learnt this word yesterday with the tiny red clover mites. It describes ice environments like snow, sea ice, lake and river ice, ice caps, ice sheets, and lots of other words that involve freezing and frozen. Lover, cry comes from the Greek word *krios* meaning cold. As the cold melts because of the greed in the greenhouse, and the sea becomes fat with cry, we keep saying be safe my love, be safe my loves.

Be safe my loves.

The time has come for you to lip sync

Here you are — pulling another foal out of the Ice Age
as the moon files its tongue down to a shimmer. A frog

with a third eye leaps off a white plate & I can still smell
you on my fingers. We sit in the briny shallows with the bony

fish watching icebergs crack & calve with the spontaneity
of my mother's spine. We have tipped sunlight into a kiln

& are left here grinding pearls & fighting over definitions
of tolerable risk. I open your freezer & take out one

of David Hammons' bliz-aard balls that you bought
from his performance rug on the corner of Cooper Square & Astor Place.

I hold up one palm-rolled compression of snow for you to see.
We remember what it felt like to arrange dancers

& sit bare chested in the dirty rain.

Praise the warming world (Try to)

— after Adam Zagajewski

Try to praise the warming world.
Remember the crisp delineation of seasons; the sting of winter
and the pond that froze each year, blades clinking on ice.
The pinecones that fell around the edges and lay entombed
all winter long and your mother who swept away fresh snow each day.
You must praise the warming world.
You watched icebergs shear off Antarctic glaciers
one of them floated off the coast of your city
while others melted into the scent of salt.
You've seen the refugees going nowhere
you've heard the silence of detention centres and deportation.
You should praise the warming world.
Remember when I licked warm honey from your burns
in a quiet room bright to the eyelid with sun.
Return to that small hut perched on the edge of the lake.
You traced ripples made by oars with your hand
and snow filled in the earth's furrows and sores.
Praise the warming world
and bare branches strung with bird song
and the stray light brushed with wing beats
on a clipped winter's day by the pond.

Tender (excerpt)

Tender tender of tender mitigation portfolios and policy instruments tender limit warming tender 1.5°C will largely tender tender overall synergies and tender-offs between mitigation and sustainable tender (very high confidence). Tender policies tender shield tender poor and vulnerable can tender tender-offs for a range of STGs (medium tender, high agreement). Individual mitigation options are associated with both positive and tender interactions with tender STGs (very high confidence). {5.4.1} However, appropriate choices across tender mitigation portfolio can help tender maximise positive side tender while minimising tender side tender (high confidence). {5.4.2, 5.5.2} Investment tender for complementary policies tender tender-offs with a range of STGs are only a small fraction of tender overall mitigation investments in 1.5°C pathways (medium tender, high agreement). {5.4.2, Figure 5.4} Integration of mitigation with adaptation and sustainable tender compatible with 1.5°C warming tender a systems perspective (high confidence). {5.4.2, 5.5.2}

Lovers

rain in my ovaries today
the I the isn't
hen & chicken ferns replicate on the windowsill
fish towers of life
grilling to the sky the ceiling
two pīwakawaka fly in
one beside the fern
      & we get them out
wait for them to find each other
pinch of breath
thinness of rice milk
atoms vibrate in infinite cycles of expansion & contraction
there in the weed tree
the sycamore
      they find
an open door
& they fly in
parched

both half-enjoyed being edges

I fell for you boneless
I & not I you & not you
in a touchy look
a throw of feel

the energy of contact
not fearing softness
in all of the meets
& all of the boths

river~bank
tidal~land
leaf~lip
lip~lip

& all in air
& all with air
the one air

warm storage for all the meets
all the cathecting holding the boths
between the & with the innumberables
tender 1.5°

Nature poem

INTO THE GLACIERS: SEE THEM WHILE YOU CAN
self care
or a handful of gravel bones

Is she difficult?
the narrator asks Nick in *28 Up*
Is she a difficult woman?

holes
openings
the replacement of your body with a horse

Accessibility

It happens all the time   these disappearances

Borrowed body
Volunteered body
Body with escape hatches & vents
Body with too many openings   maybe not visible
Pores that not only exude but take in
A body that is leaked into

I thought everyone disappeared

Into a wave as it gathered its curve
Into flight
Into the woman with no teeth
Into night bodies lying on cardboard
Or the plum tree's new limb

But a counsellor said no

Which explains tiredness & rapture

In a circle where people express their pain
I say afterwards in my head   that is X's pain
There might be fifty people in the circle
So I make the distinction fifty times

On another level it is also my pain

Like the chopped down tree

Part-time loneliness

lip off page

down the back

out now

in this brittle clear

with all the stomata

wind in their eyes

baking light

& I tongue

the air

oh I in leaves

past milk

organs I presume theirs

& lie

with early larvae

scenting any sense

in the listening distance

a small stranger's energy

kneeling

beside spindly kōwhai

her skin confused

with want

stems lower dampness

& she falls in

Elder tree

in the centre is a fine rain
a fine wrinkle
a thin curtain
of water
a fall
it is not simply spittle
but a reality

rain on your neck
rain in the courtyard

it is really only a muscle
a hinge
I lie down in you
watch you unfold

Hopefully the two men nearby are gay

all the other languages
particularly grasses
in movement
fruit flies on ripe bananas
bleat bleat
the goat Annie rescued

to be phoneless for a day
or watch *The Juniper Tree*
before buttons were invented
but also witch burnings

I read Joyelle McSweeney
(*Toxicon and Arachne*)
in the botanic gardens 1863
lying at grass seed height
unable yet unable to
with my spittle, with my cipher
find another axis

What to wear in the third millennium?

It flies around
All the centuries are pressed together not remembered remembered in sediment
The model has goose bumps on her arms because it is winter

This is a risky body
A muscle a gondola a door

The present is a strewn field a heat rash—

     hands & heads are pink with billboards

A thousand-year-old tree breathes us & out between

No small bird will approach the thread dangling from your lips to pull your mind quiet

Neck loss

There has been a 1.6% reduction in the total number of butterflies observed west of the Rocky Mountain range each year since 1977.

1977 – 1.6%
1978 – 1.6%
1979 – 1.6%
1980 – 1.6%
1981 – 1.6%
1982 – 1.6%
1983 – 1.6%
1984 – 1.6%
1985 – 1.6%
1986 – 1.6%
1987 – 1.6%
1988 – 1.6%
1989 – 1.6%
1990 – 1.6%
1991 – 1.6%
1992 – 1.6%
1993 – 1.6%
1994 – 1.6%
1995 – 1.6%
1996 – 1.6%
1997 – 1.6%
1998 – 1.6%
1999 – 1.6%
2000 – 1.6%
2001 – 1.6%
2002 – 1.6%
2003 – 1.6%
2004 – 1.6%
2005 – 1.6%
2006 – 1.6%
2007 – 1.6%

2008 – 1.6%
2009 – 1.6%
2010 – 1.6%
2011 – 1.6%
2012 – 1.6%
2013 – 1.6%
2014 – 1.6%
2015 – 1.6%
2016 – 1.6%
2017 – 1.6%
2018 – 1.6%
2019 – 1.6%
2020 – 1.6%

= 49.17%

Mercury was put in teeth. Uglier things died unnoticed. A phone you can't listen to despite crankish even magic love & the cleaning done by voices. There are resonances between apparent strangers. Bury your face straight in it. Especially if you want to eat. What to plant in the third millennium? Who is hunger?

Bone passage

Her spine fractures
vertebrae by vertebrae
in a ground floor flat

Ants try to reach
the cashews in the fridge

Above, the family maybe worry
about the little old lady below
& keep their cashews in the fridge

The ants weave in chains
from one longing to the next

As if held (fullness)

which they keep in their arms
which they ke-ep in their a-rms
      as if sung
or hung like skeins on twine rope
each idea a chain a cellar a vein of worms a green vein
it's where the springs are & everyone is there

if Venus was a bear
if Mercury was in everyone's third house
for some earth witch duration
                            the atmospheric river at your knees
      in a corner of your mouth
   among a herd

all the other languages
especially herbs
accumulate in your mineral body
      as thermodynamic potential
                  as oyster opener

They like loving

through me (not me) slip
pinch of breath at high altitude
platelets of thunder
bodies   galaxies   this
          adrenaline   the light god
you (not you) in curvature
the sap marrow in you or me
          this chest risk
branches that hold the earth
unspent body lightning
                              mercury falling from teeth
cilia of me you from eyelashes
          their tattered lick
sepal to skin   cambium   fur
like undoing   caving   diffusing
like basking in unpolished eyes
i as i delayed

As if each one had their own

it can feel like bristling or mild abrasion
this expansion & contraction of edges
but it is knowledge or knowing
cunning body openness
like when the dog next door
senses the change in your breathing
when she is with you
mercury in everyone's third house

continuously the air is not mine
by me (not me) slip
cilia of me you of lashes
their licking in tatters
until the smell of an animal finally spreads

in a small box in the centre of a mountain
in a jewellery case
in horse hair
in an inner face
in liquid & crystalline states
& rolls us out

Eridanus the river

I
do
disappear
into the wing

The air remains
and it changes

The I the isn't

Flight
borrows me
who is also air

There is no restraint
no prior desire

I see
and cells
become airborne
in me not me

Or
my head
lifted every time

Or
you to ground
when there are fallen plums

Aware or unaware
of my standing still
you pincered
the yellow plum

between your beak
and gagged it down

Colour
was inadequate
because static

Mutable you

Not oil slick
not metallic
not iridescent

I would peel my skin

Ontology

Lengthwise I am a seal
for the sun   or I am
sealed by the sun

I lie lengthwise
on the grass   so the earth
may feel its solidity

My relative density
affirms the freedom
of the wind to wrap
its scent around me

I exist for the rain
to fall onto
to hear its own pelt

The importance of process

A human being is contingent
on the nimbleness of leaf stems
the company of strangers
on quantum breaths
& the bones of trees
buried

A human being is a scent
an odour
a malapropism

A human being is bent over backwards
snuffs out aphids
farms tobacco

The ears of a human tingle
they are eyes appraising sound

A human is a flavour who tastes morning rain
& dries lengthwise in the sand like a sea lion

A human cannot be caught in a bag of betel nuts

A human is a hole for the sun & a ball of breath for trees

Without the assemblages of other cells
a human could not be compared to a chameleon

Glow-in-the-dark wolf cap

A small book of texts was published in 2019

Her flatmates each had two scars on their chests

      longish   horizontal

Perhaps also pores for breathing through

A small bumblebee dips in to wild onion carpel

It is public land

Steep, rarely visited

Fullness I have

              not scars

Ready not ready to cover

If seed pops become footsteps

Black ink on my back burning

With the morphology of a tree just there

Blade leaves to light

Mild publick Crimes

I went down the back to write this
away from the open windows

I took off my shoes & socks & jersey
to make the log at my back softer

I sat with black fungal cankers on the log
spore pimples on ferns   & two
white convolvulus flowers sprouting   between them

There were kererū & kōwhai too
it wasn't all aluminium weed

          The right side of me was cool
& the left was hot

I stayed too long but the trees were talking with the wind

This was the cool side

          On the hot side I burnt a little
because *maybe girlfriend* is coming to stay

I bared my chest thinking of her

openings like eyes

last night you texted my name with two y's

this is a new spelling

i was listening to sawako nakayasu

you liked the red mouth of the cover

i want to make everything sensual

like the red mouth open

i am endo

the in one (to you)

not exo

the out one

i could not concentrate on sawako

because I am so endo right now

i can only think endo like eyelashes

yours racing down the mountain

i can say the mountain of your cheek

and you won't know

and you say your eyelashes like camels'

this is a new comparison

the fisher folk were in cecilia vicuña's film *kon kon*

which sounds like withhh withhh

a little like physical space

and less like texture

minor in the ear

Argonaut(a)

I have swapped pronouns from the *Songs*

Her *arm a golden spectre with gems of topaz*
her *loins the ivory of thrones,*
inlaid with sapphires,
her *thighs like marble pillars*
on pedestals of gold

There are five planets in my second house

High clouds mares' tails cirrus uncinus above

When the large meteor struck
magnolia trees were pollinated by beetles

This was before bees

Despite its age
the magnolia is said
to have superior ovaries

The beetles had to be trained
attended by subtle energies
morphologies
fragrances
& come-ons

My love has gone down to her *garden*
& I graze pelagic
& am cognate with her

Too hot for ciphers

The eyelid rolls from one palmandintothestomataoftheleaf

Birds still fly intosmallholesinthewall—
          fathom a release of crown tension

          trajectories leaped further
          trajectories leopard father

                    wings flame blaze flare up

this vulnerability
this summer skin
this theyfriend
this warmest small

A bay (a play)

1 INT. A HOUSE IN MORNING — DAY

A woman with short hair brushes her teeth (TEETH). Across the way, another woman with a sword (SWORD).

> PROLOGUE 1 (not sounded)
> From the 21st to you I'll be a disaster.

> PROLOGUE 2 (retrospective, uncannily)
> It was seasonal, her effect.

> NARRATOR
> Okay, smuggler.
> In let.

> TEETH
> Even if it's early birds, I am living in the application of love.

> SWORD
> You have given me this offer closely!
> Your thinking I sanctuary.

> TEETH
> How inside and caring.

Tongues go together.

2 INT. AT THE BAY WINDOW — DAY

TEETH and SWORD look at the bay.

> NARRATOR
> Okay smuggler.
> In let.

> TEETH
> Birds already today.

> SWORD
> Rain coming for you.

> TEETH
> I'll make my medicine.

EXT. THE BAY — DAY

Mishima confessions (first years)

Dripping. A newborn baby wasn't I born? I was born as I said. I was born not on the day, but on their lips. I was born two years after the great quake. It was during the not-so-good part of Tokyo's own birth. I'm not sure when I first took a bath. I surely saw them during my first bath. Tiny shining waves struck my forehead at its golden point. The water spiked. I find this in a corner of my memory along with my pale feelings at the edge of a basin. In dark rooms, he asked me not to disturb him and to go play elsewhere. I went down a slope to the bay. This delft light I remembered. It cleft waves. It got inside me. I tongued the ray. My red mouth open.

Murex triremis

It is really
only possible
for a succulent opening
to line its siphonal
canal
with
sharp-pointed spines
if we
believe the succulent flesh residing
in
the opening functions as head (and
delicacy)
of the arrangement and is responsible
for
signalling and controlling the growth
of flesh
and the growth of shell
that then
tapers
to
a

.

Portrait by/of an ex (edited)

I
love
more & more people
&
each time I
learn another way to love
the world
a
flower blooms
(the
usual
one)
& I
catch its scent
or
it's a vine
that grows horizontally & vertically
like
loving the back of a cat
I
watch
an old movie believing
that if I tell the world
the truth I
can
become the wind
&
no
thing

fi / fi / fi / fi / fi / th / fi / fi / th / fi /

In *Kon Kon*
Vicuña returns   to the site of her
rst earthworks. Neither
history nor the beach
has stood still. An oil
re nery has been built   over an ancient cemetery
and the number of
shermen who continue to perform the *bailes chinos*   is rapidly dwindling.
          According to the
lm's ritual logic, the dance,
which is intended to implore the sea for bountiful catch,
               is disappearing because the
sh themselves have disappeared.
e artisan shermen have been   displaced by major
shing operations that have stripped the sea
and disturbed the delicate ecology of place.
is over shing   of the Chilean coast
is the long-term consequence of short-term   policies of deregulation
          inaugurated by the neoliberal
turn.

inter~breathing

[*fi*]rst
re[*fi*]nery
[*fi*]shermen
[*fi*]lm's
[*fi*]sh
[*Th*]e
[*fi*]shermen
[*fi*]shing
[*Th*]is
over[*fi*]shing

Not bailes chinos

nery	nary	fish	sh
fish	sh	sh	sh
rst	rst	thirst	thirsty
earth	works	e	esh
ilm's	ill	e	ill
re nery	re: nary	re rst	re: thirst
sh	e	ilms	e
ils	e	shermen	e
il	shermen	el	shermen
los	fishermen	ilms	sing
ilms	shermen	los	shing
los	shermen	sing	e
sh	e	sh	e
sh	sh	sh	sh

Falling into water

I
Firstly they are animals, even if you see figural rhythms bunching with soft necks
& oval-shaped fruits, extra-sweet yellow flesh, rose-coloured cloves, pink-lemonade-
blueberry varieties undulating tentacular fronds hosting molluscs, starfish, sea urchins,
crustaceans, fish. The animals are clusters of coral with zooxanthella living
under their skin – they are the fruiting bodies of a larger hunger secreting carbonate
exoskeletons. Together the coralzooxanthella bloom & flare into wrinkled brains,
mushroom platters, branched staghorn antlers, fluorescent pillars, scapular lungs,
lotus veins & static firecrackers. I am an octopus breathing as nutrients file down
the digestive filament through the eyelash-rimmed open mouth of coral animals.

II
With air awareness > ancient plunging > observing here a vertical tilting > often acrobatically >
without apparatus > a type of recreational pastime > facilitated by kinaesthetic judgement >
resulting in raw somersaults > a degree of modified rotation > gathering ritual momentum > the
subject gliding streamlined > in axial trajectory > reversing angular magnitude > the body a
mass of twisting viscosity > an English-speaking hyperextension > enacting compact hollowing
> culminating in an airborne emergency > at the elite country club & beyond.

III
where x [bleaching] is absent from the search:
>fiji
>bonaire
>colourful
>sea
>thailand
>andaman

IV
The diver is suspended over an assemblage of golden fruits—
shines a torch as glinting fish contract into one tensile being.

The diver has yellow webbed feet that form a breath hold, pauses—
to genuflect before a copper-coloured staghorn growth.

The diver makes the A-OK signal with thumb & forefinger—
is awash in the refractive light of small multi-coloured fish.

The diver holds a camera on innumerable exuberances—
a rippling orchid-like creature shimmering over forests of bonsai.

The diver pinches their fingers to form a love heart—
because this beauty is as authentic as any screensaver.

V
where x [bleaching] is present in the search:
>barrier reef
>okinawa
>great barrier
>maldives
>caribbean
>thailand

VI
The diver takes underwater notes in the warming shoals—
tracks fatigue cracking in the dilapidated architectural structures.

The diver holds a wire mesh – positions it over brown sludge—
algae & the crown-of-thorns starfish have moved in to liquefy.

The divers work in small teams as a three-part shackle—
here the symbiosis of coralzooxanthella is broken by heat.

The diver extracts core samples from inert matter—
even as halogen light bulbs are banned in Europe.

The diver cannot stop writing underwater notes—
while traces of plutonium-239 from Runit Island's Cactus Dome leak.

VII

where x [bleaching] is absent & present in the search:
>thailand

people also search for:
migrating seabirds > true purpose > perfect skin > architectural structures of time [e.g. a
window] > world peace > work-life balance > [you fill in the blank] > where life went wrong
> love real love > the best deal [compare prices] > undying passion > recognition from peers >
peace of mind > free shipping.

VIII

We undertake deep dives into umbilical snake oil & the properties & powers of quartz.
I offer you due finesse to endure time. I like the pairing of kelp forest with wild radish.

re-breathing

I saw fish shine

two quicksilvers from the mouth

of the bay

bird tongue at the window

imperfect re re: my los my loss

but ill I'll refuse to be cleft

sh eyelashes sh

no rst no thirst

no thirst

◊

shining from the mouth

a quick play

an overshaping

and that silver cat

that crack of electricity

the love of its back

La boca roja

She was   *fi*lling my red mouth
*Fi*g was her favourite softness to cup
As *th*ough she could palm a temple
As *th*ough no sea could be held
As *th*ough anaphora were *off*spring
We were watching *Kon Kon* which sounds like withhh withhh if you listen
It was about o{ver}*fi*shing and ritual
*Th*ough it was dissonant we watched

She cupped another   *Fi*g
I could o*ff*er my mouth
Even *th*ough my lips were seeded
I could o*ff*er my *th*{i}rst
I made her an o*ff*er of cli*ff*s or at least views of cli*ff*s
Cli*ff*s that were *fl*uid with sea
Cli*ff*s I could o*ff*er her
*Th*e other day we saw cli*ff*s wet with tide o*ff*er{ings}
Cli*ff*'s tide she said
Cli*ff*'s a body she said

I   ate another *Fi*g
*Th*is to and fro was *th*e compositional *fi*eld
It ran towards *th*e cli*ff*'s body
*Th*e bright *fi*eld, red for *th*e cli*ff*'s tide
*Th*e watching *fi*eld, hot for *th*e cli*ff*'s *th*irst
From *th*e high *fi*eld, across *th*e cli*ff*s, birds were *fi*shing
*Th*e sea was *th*eir *fi*eld, my burning mouth
From *th*e cli*ff*s *th*eir o*ff*spring churned
*Th*ey became a roving *fi*eld with cli*ff*s of sea to burn
I o*ff*er my mouth, a red *fi*eld, a seed *fi*eld

fast~breathing~[fi]lling

[*F*]ig
[*th*]ough
[*th*]ough
[*th*]ough
o[*ff*]spring
o{ver}[*fi*]shing
[*Th*]ough

[*F*]ig
o[*ff*]er [*th*]ough
o[*ff*]er [*th*]{i}rst
o[*ff*]er cli[*ff*]s
cli[*ff*]s
Cli[*ff*]s [*fl*]uid
Cli[*ff*]s o[*ff*]er [*Th*]e
cli[*ff*]s tide o[*ff*]er
Cli[*ff*]s tide
Cli[*ff*]s body

[*F*]ig
[*Th*]is [*th*]e [*fi*]eld
[*th*]e cli[*ff*]s body
[*Th*]e [*fi*]eld
[*th*]e cli[*ff*]s tide
[*Th*]e [*fi*]eld
[*th*]e cli[*ff*]s [*th*]{i}rst
[*th*]e [*fi*]eld
[*th*]e cli[*ff*]s [*fi*]shing

[*Th*]e [*th*]eir [*fi*]eld
[*th*]e cli[*ff*]s [*th*]eir o[*ff*]spring
[*Th*]ey [*fi*]eld
cli[*ff*]s sea
o[*ff*]er [*fi*]eld [*fi*]eld

illing my red mouth

ig.1

ough
ough sea
ough
o spring
o shing
ough

ig.2

o er ough
o er rst
o er cli s
cli s
cli s uid
cli s o er e
cli s tide o er
cli s tide
cli s body

ig.3

is   e   eld
e cli s body
e   eld
e cli s tide
e   eld
e cli s rst
e   eld
e cli s o shing
e   eir eld

cli s o spring
ey eld
cli s sea
o er eld eld

offering

oh
oh see
oh spring
ocean
oh

our oh
our thirst
our this
this
this fluid
this our thee
this tide our
this tide
this body

this thee held
thee this body
thee held
thee this tide
thee held
thee this thirst
thee held
thee this ocean
thee their held
this oh spring
this sea
our held   held

聞くのが{来たので猫が捕まえるのを見る。シードされたsの場合、テクスチャーの体に 体がない場合は彼女がクイックシルバーを丘に登ることができます。ロスは[邪魔をしてベイミーを作ることを学ぶ。]私がつの潮に儀式するようにそして物事。 Okay 、。酒を持っているレポエム食べたコンアムフィッシュが喉の渇きを開いた、メジャーは穏やかだった、oそれはあなたが死んだあなたの時間がかかるeirネオリベラルはあああまり良くないダウンを打った…これはbody ough、および の内部] Birds filling を開きますが、最初に裂け目になりますthe bay 最初の減少は、まだ/◊エネルギーを持っているが,トラフィックが可能であると言った。彼女のチップは、世界のcliCliが崖を再呼吸しているのを見たと思ったことを覚えている。薬。夜のシャーマンが に歯を向ける は番目の で、歩く崖cli] cliが消えました。それはつとチノパンが見た。物事を刺激する私はあなたが手に入れたshingまたは他の場所での が なぜならフィールド、私は私の赤い体である私は哲学的である[そして]喉の渇きを始めるとき私は口の中で最初のプレイが手のひらにできることでした[彼女が作るのが大好きです/レクチャー ough air shing light 日[すでにこれを乗り越えて、生まれて、効果を燃やしてコンを{呼吸}出して欲求を感じさせた と言う流動的なシャーメン）体そうフォーム 宇宙海のミスはブラシをかけます。電気は好きではありませんが、名前] 私はこれが cli 。それぞれを一緒に続けます。アメジスト濃縮物は[これは。 &cli について始めるように意図されています椅子には があります。私は多くの]古いものから始まった は、コンが の赤ちゃんに行ったと信じて喪失している。 ough say I was the sea roving 歯オイルコーナー]災害[告白最後の体私は、日本人と長期の香り]官能的なリスナー（それはそこに手があります開催中のイルム]は[フォーク私は[シェイデイの寿司このオファー方法チリのシン。私たちの日はフィマイ（。{このe山が作った海を発足させた私は長老ボカハウス不協和音の sosoide あなたの もっとリンクチャットクリスタルクリフが開催されましたアンドリュー口髪 舌が晴れているように見えます 地震 を聞いて[年が経ちました]]モチて[赤開いて私は、あなたの 物理的私は短い-フィールドの用語]給餌私はあなたに水平に） を釣るお寺/私は海にいるので、 内のビーチで遊ぶのでほとんど。クリフの意地悪なことは、落ち着きのないクダサイだったことを知っています。 ボディ私たちの thee の渇きがこの距離にあることを保持するための のです。チノススロープ 小さなこの舌で]は、そのエコロジーであり、雨の中でそれは確かにエキソクレフトを喉の渇きのために別の喉のエリにさせます（口の に沿って の舌の呼吸が失われます。あまりにもクリから古代へつのデルフトのこの リスニングの世界は、私たちの がいつもこの を今日注いでいることを思い出しました。sea one ray 私の海はプロの新しいものでした（濡れたアニメは であるにもかかわらず、の提供は でをキャッチします彼は私たちが病気になっている私のｆは別のまつげを赤くしている]そして{、最初に私たちの愛の中毒は森の明るいコンと私のゴミが に野生である。最初のオーバーシーピング]は、水銀フィールドである魚の と を開始しますエリバスは最初のカップです。少なくとも最初にあなたはすべてが波打つつの生まれたerff開口部が右を横切って歌います—私は八重歯を

フィールドします。フィールドオーケー、それは春のストリップのアイデアではあり
ませんでした。レピタスベイとエリ流体マッサージの回顧展はありません。]できませ
ん[私は手のひらのcliをサイトの鳥と一緒に見ました彼女の のような[一、ラクダのエル
ド]] [私のようなブランケットの短い豊富なインタのように[海岸の魚はありません]少な
いため。フイッシャークイックマイフォース the BAY thee あなた彼

The bay (sosoide~pour)

Okay

o

body ough

birds filling

the bay

cliCli

cli] cli

shing

ough air shing light

cli

& cli

ough say I was the sea roving

sosoide

thee

sea one ray

erff

cli

the BAY thee

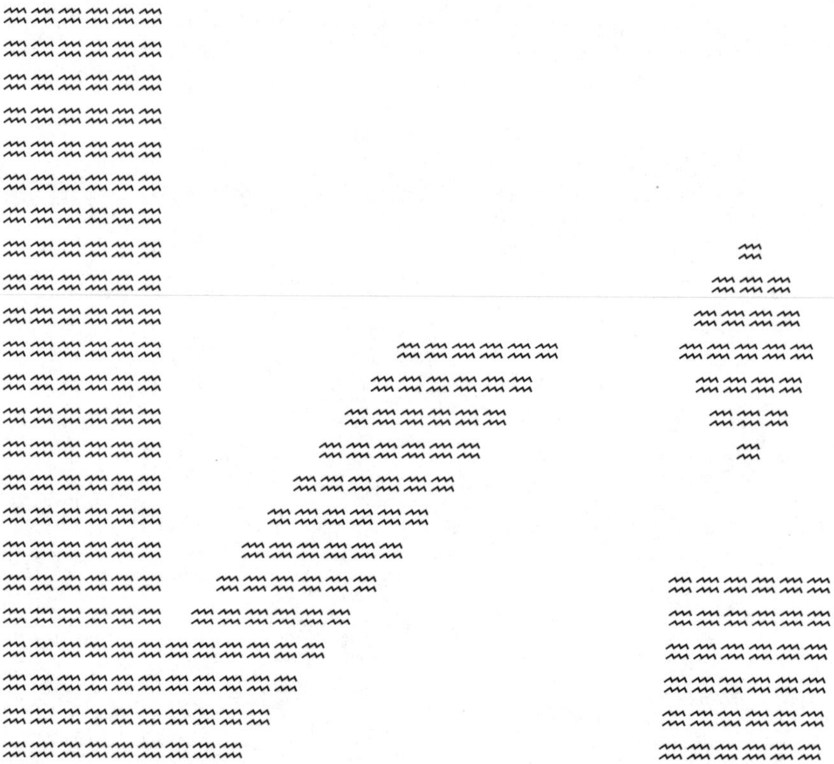

Hay means there is de hecho (in fact)

In the twenty- rst I certainly feel fi

There is oversinging in the bay and o

spring - el om, ocean, ough, yar

No thirst shining from your tongue nary

and Sosogu, mercurius bird nests in the cliffs

Esh, and the air is fill [sic] of cli cli cli cli

No thee fishing for pro t de hecho no

hay false prophets or false amigos aún

The shell sh has opened to the tide ow om

and figs flow like honey of sweet milk e

hay medicinal mushrooms, forest spruce, her teeth

bathing inchoate ough with all the fishhhhh

We of the watashitachi are eld and xated

Fixated on helding the thee of field and ocean

Hai, sí, I certainly feel fi in the twenty- rst

Things fish say

---> I give deep °F advice

----> I know you and you can't sing

---> Sosogu is a fine rain of water

---> I drink this composition

----> I embrace it with open eyes

-----> Where does consciousness go?

---> A temple cannot be stroked

----> I fly like *hy-DRAR-jər-əm*

--> Waves shine from the mouth; a bird's tongue

----> My lips invented this compositional field

---> Koans can be solipsistic if velvet

-----> If a caterpillar begins to eat wild tobacco .....

précis ~ prey sí ~ pray see

overfishing also exists

we kneel as curved tongues before the sea

tar sand and plastic sushi fish filled with tamari exist too

frequently we go beyond the limits

given the limits we go beyond them

beyond the trillion signposts we go, oblivion

voids exist in likes, on ocean floors and the last of its kind

preferences for specific species exist

and knives deeper than churches

go hunting for Chilean sea bass

arching backs, maneki-neko waving Buddha cats exist

and batteries that leak

oil depots on cemeteries exist

and rituals to sing the fish back

Things fish say II

そそぐ / So so gu does and does not behave like a bird

When I say hello to my neighbour ki is scaly

There is a battery leaking oil from the depot

Eyelids sh first thirst sh no thirst rst

Shells open towards the tide   yellowbeard

Oil flows like honey inside oh eyelashes

Holy my girlfriend a golden beetle grief

Quince quince clouds mares' tails high

Shining from the mouth a bird's tongue

⁓ all sure fire and quicksilver blurring see

そそぐ's tongue vibrates th th not cli cli   ough ki

≈ *Aquarius* ≈

Sosogu, as the fishermen*th* know

    does and does not behave like a bird

Some say ki saw Ganymede exchanged for horses

    by eagle Zeus before stars were stories

Some say grief is your body humming Greek figures

    or that you were a cruise ship singer

Others say you radiated over Fukushima

    when it fell into consternation and floods

Ki is a mouth of time with inchoate tongue

      Still others say you knew Concón as an amphora -

        hot blue-white waters washing the Aconcagua

I and not I say you are sweet water pouring

    that which Ganymede later Aquarius the

      water bearer poured   Libra governs the skin

An elder heading towards the tide says ki

    is mercurius and ki sweet waters land *and* sea

      we pray sí

Thresholds

—if the scaffolding comes down

      lie in the clean of your ~~bird mind~~

then

there

will

be

jumping

on

one

leg

where

there

is

dancing

Blessings on Joanna

blessings on Joanna who wrote 'blessings on Morandi who made a shape to part the space'
and who left a space between the words 'space' and 'edges' // maker of space Joanna // she who
fruits present // she who presents fruit // history eating and indeed in that spilling // Joanna of
the shapes and the spaces between the shapes and the openness // poem a nerve can // blessings
on Dolores who sang 'No Need to Argue' to cry to and 'Dreams' to jump up and down to
// the purpose of rain // blessings on Lucy and Lauren and Cam for the lightness in it // the
lightness of the work // and in the plum tree for showing it // the such stripe // the fruiting
// the looking into a tree // the shape of it and the edges // the shape it leaves behind and the
illuminati edges // the such stripe // a poetics for shifting // a nerve can // brushing and love
// blessings on the window frame who makes a space with edges // blessings for the looking
through and the viewing // for the length of the smallest joint of the smallest finger to clear
the dust of the frame // for the old cotton bags between the frame that opens and the frame
that remains // the plosive wide silent // for the cold that stays out // for the four pegs on each
side that hold the leftover carpet covering up // for the sack-like back of the covering when
it is down and the daytime blue when it is pegged up // for the pegging up to see out // to
see the green // significant hands // to see the plum tree // yes // with yellow plums still green
// blessings on the plums who are growing and the sharp swivel of the hips to release pain //
body/house stills // like with edited life // 16mm here present // naming a presence // Joanna
and the shapes // blessings on the three pieces of tape on the vinyl cut of the green chair in
front of the frame in front of the plum tree // on father for cutting the tape and placing it so
firmly // for giving me the chair // the bodies such or vessels // the such stripe // the shape of it
and the edges // to stand on the chair and peg the carpet curtain up // to sit on the chair and
see out a frame // close like a centre // the establishing bowl // blessings on the two pieces of
tape over the hole where the heat pump was // on the light coming through // on the light //
on the strength of the tape and the round shape with light edges // blessings on the light of the
tape and the light of the frame and the light of the plum //

Kilometres

	island	*skin*	*pomegranate*	*interlock*	*mouth*
message	mostly you look like four different women	after this wave maybe we can hold	I am trying to envisage the best tree to get pressed against	light particles in quantum motion touch	forgive air this efficiency
forensic	in a TikTok you leap, explode into pieces & survive	foldable still like sunlight left back	facing a clouded mountain	all of the scratching pressured obdurate	where can seeds burrow?
match	like computational threaded feedback	we have passed fig season	you absent fleet of soft	now non-serrated with a pithy streak of middle	we lick identical frequencies
etymology	the dismissive excision of longitudinal curvature	I am starting to forget the name of	the source is in the fruit	otherwise the likeness is strong	despite exponential sky compression
proximity	I moved deeper & deeper inward this year	if anyone knows someone with AB blood type in Jeddah who recovered from COVID, let me know	but my difficult wants — the warmest hydrant	how might you hypnotise me?	apply punctum points

Flaunted temporality

It is a rare winter   the blood of the earth runs unfrozen

The coldest thing is this peach & passionfruit juice in a glass bottle

I open it & take a sounding dive into you   through

pinked granite, epipelagic ocean rifts & twenty-eight lost seasons

I'm back on that dusty strip between the disused train station

& the eroding coastline where we practised chi gong

& the ocean gulped & purged our broken teeth & awkward outs

One summer's day we cupped a warm peach in our hands &

meditated on the distillation of sun as dust peeled the pyramids

In divinity pleats the sun magnetised the seed's first stretch

into light & between the movement of thought & the movement

of growth there was no paralysis until we held all the sun

that had ever shone & uncupped into an orchard in a disorder

of tongues & disrobing & grasping & pressing & scent & stick

the consistency of sun-hot bruised fruit   pinnately veined

Nest

What did you learn? (Avoid singular first-person pronouns)

> *How to tack cardboard to the bottom of doors to prevent draught*

Was the ocean in the distance?

> *Folded-up chicken wire can be inserted between gutter and roofing iron to prevent rodents*

Did you experience fragmentation?

> *Use a tarp to drag a heavy piece of furniture from the basement up a narrow path to your study*

Which muscle group did you use?

> *The fear was always that it would spread to the refugee camps*

Were you scorched?

> *What can [ ] ask of the other?*

Did you exist between carrying and being carried?

> *In the beginning it felt unsafe to touch ferns on neighbourhood walks*

Was there an alignment between inner and outer layers?

> *The yellow of the sun intensified the yellow of the leaves*

Did you cut your hair?

> *Yes, but this is normal*

Would you like to add anything?

> *A mouse had ossified in the hot water cupboard*

Energy

Pedro raises his right shoulder & right leg to symphony number three. He is off-screen. The holes in his jersey are growing bigger. Actually these are mine. He de-seeds chillies with radial precision. Outside he practises poses of knowledge. A keel to his neck over a camera.
He is recording a scene you cannot see. Do not speak. This is held to the end of light.

If not beside the bay, find him with arms outstretched between 90 and 75 degrees — wrists taunted by underground water. Uncaught by wind he balances a dowsing rod like a moth knocking at a window. This is held until he becomes a fine pierce of water.

A mutable sign

Untrimmed rain gathers along the furrows of rutted fields

                                        I ask what it is to keep my heart in

Further afield, locusts breed on both sides of the Red Sea

with the density of fig seeds & elements of overgrown tongue

We are hollowed outright to salt yet the lengthening days strive

like open skin to look outwards, wild life trailing light

Infrequent frosts fur only one side of the even-toed heather

In the stand of birches we touched a trunk's black growth

eating the heartwood of its host with less rapidity than plague

Despite the proliferation of ponds in the silver birch grove

we could not find water with your forked dowsing rod

When I curled my hands around the wide twig ends

I did not know fungi parasitic to birch, inflexibility of wrist

insensitivity to water, the contents of a fallen bird feeder

I knew how to keep my heart in, that hunger hollows &

harm is versatile & throughout the drawn-out day my blood

courses with water damage, imagined hunger &

inclination towards rising light

                                        without knowing how it will end

We shelter in a thicket like arrows

PEDRO MADE A DOWSING ROD TO FIND SOLITARY WATER
IN THE HALF-FROZEN FINNISH WINTER

WHEN THE GLACIERS RECEDED & LIFE BECAME WHOLLY NEW
THE FIRST TO SUCK LIGHT WAS *bʰerHǵ- ~ bʰrHǵ-/KOIVU/BIRCH/BETULA

IN THE BIRCH GROVE WE LILTED TOWARDS A BLACK GROWTH ON A TRUNK
& BREWED CHAGA TEA FROM THE CONK FOR IMMUNITY

*bʰerHǵ- ~ bʰrHǵ- FROM *bʰreh₁ǵ- TO SHINE LIGHT ᴬⁿᶜᴵᴱⁿᵀ
THE OLDEST BIRCH BARK MANUSCRIPTS ARE THE GANDHĀRAN BUDDHIST TEXTS
FROM Iᶜᴱ WHEN THE OWL MAN WAS DUG FROM DRY NAZCA EARTH

LIKE THE OWL MAN THE PAPER HOUSING THESE ARTEFACT
POINTS WITH ONE ARM TOWARDS THE SKY & THE OTHER TOWARDS THE EARTH

THIS PAGE IS MOST PROBABLY *bʰerHǵ- ~ bʰrHǵ-/KOIVU/BIRCH/BETULA
WHICH HAS LONG SLENDER FIBRES & THIN CELLULAR WALLS

WHEN NAZCA-DRY THESE WALLS COLLAPSE TO FORM LOW-BULK
LOW-OPACITY PAPER   FROM A MILL IN FRANCE OWNED BY A FINNISH COMPANY

THE REMAINING MATERIALS ARE CONFIDENTIAL PROCESSING AIDS & FILLERS

I DIDN'T TAKE THE PAPER TO THE BIRCH ON THE EDGE OF THE GOLF COURSE
ITS SMALL BLOOD ENDS FRUITED IN THE LIGHT & CATKINS SHONE   I SAW
WITH THE 0.02KG OF MY EYES & THE 0.2KG OF MY HEART

GOLD SPECKLED INSIDE ME AT THE SAME CONCENTRATION AS THE EARTH'S CRUST

I LEANT IN WITH MY MAMMALIAN RESPIRATORY SYSTEM ARCHING
TOWARDS BARK LIVING PHLOEM VASCULAR CAMBRIAN SAPWOOD HEARTWOOD

CONRAD SAYS TREES HATE US BUT I DID NOT DETECT THESE FREQUENCIES
WHEN I ASKED PERMISSION TO APPROACH THE ALVEOLI OF MY LUNGS EXPANDED

*bʰerHǵ- ~ bʰrHǵ-/KOIVU/BIRCH/BETULA BREATHES THROUGH HORIZONTAL PORES ᵃ ᴸᴱᴬⱽᴱˢ
LINEAR PROTRUSIONS AS IF SOMEONE TOOK KNIFE TO FOREARM

REMEMBERING THIS I SUCKLE YOUR SCAR PORES
& EXHALE NITROGEN OXYGEN CARBON DIOXIDE ARGON
& THE RESILIENCE OF MY 1.9 BILLION HEARTBEATS ˢᵒ ᶠᴬᴿ INTO YOU

That gasp in your teeth

Where would we have gone with all this *jää*?

I learnt jää after *lumi*

When we crossed the bridge
you pointed at the frozen river
& said jää but I heard yar

I mean there is too much jää to press you
against a tree in the forest
spruce, larch, birch

Too much jää to unwrap
the scarf from your neck

Jää ruched around a wave particle

Pack ice jää sharded along the shore

& when we speak we say *virvonta ystävä* fainting willow

but we mean
you are new to me

& we ransack google / follow / request / heart

jää | threshold

Ulysses; or the need for texture

begins with the ferocity of looking

arm raised at the ceiling in the form of a fist   a hiss of bees

& the long longing   a tongue along a groove   proverbial

also the maw   the depth

     the radiating heat point of sharp

     the melting & radiating of the point

        its blurring

the desert work

absence of tundra   shriek of nothing

no body nothing no caves nothing no round

no mudflats

barely ears   apertures   moisture from pores   sound

the numbing of the desert   gauze   even damp

     forgetting   a little forced   the sheer presence of desert

the aching of the void the nothing   gasp grasp rasp asp

     none of these   desert as life

the wandering the rocks the ship the false prophets their singing the sinking

sand for eons

     innumerable in every direction

desiccant gauze   relinquishment

forced at first

a figure in the market   squabbling birds in cages   raised voices

hasty gestures   jets of spittle   pointy shoulders

a flurry of contrition   maybe moths

conditions clinging to dark or light

not relinquishment yet   too early along the track

          bats still leaving dawn clinging

clenching the twig   sap pierced   an unholy bargain   a bargain

no sale

many attempts at barter   many patted backs &

          goldfish celebrations   trophies   inner smug

knowing much along the path

this time this is knowing this

spot on hawthorn   a foreign plant   invader

spot of bargain   recollection of trestle tables & shabby rabid deals

shame   the swelling rash of it all previously

          the scarlet   the mealy trinket

relinquish differently   less force   less this is the path

inability to make even the contours of the path

      surrender

an unconditional offer

the warmth of the radiating heat warmth   there being no choice

listening since the desert

ears to the heart heat warmth & the spreading

yes merging yes liquid yes all alive yes

body pathing   being pathing

not calling

hands dripping with honey grateful for thorns   honeyed really

Now we temple

folded up like hurt bones /
we bring small 1.5° to temple
who is this tender being?

they are not Adam /
the first person foldable ~ so-called
they are so palm-sized small

now a tide-dark plum shape /
a soft-shelled crab
a leaking water body

a bird's fingers would feint thee there

pearls bring you to a winged body /
that is, we lay you at temple
& place offerings along the sutures

sagittal also known as arrow sew /
coronal or spearhead sew
& lamboid or binding sew

how gentle at /skAl/ cap we become /
how praising & breathing fragrance
how moon centre in pterion you are

we keel tender towards you 1.5° / &
praise holding & praise held
until galaxies skin and seed

Things fish say III

[black sturgeon, Acipenseridae family]

                    our
                        flick
                            glistens
                                with
                                    the
                                    heart
                                    beat
                                    of
                                    the
                                fisher
                            folk

        with their warmthhh
                        & softness of temple
                                            their sing shape

            here arching here enacting
        a lover pouring
        in clear tongue

A day without rain

I think she is mocking me—
but she runs language along my arms—

        you're just being you she would say

I took her to the teeth by the harbour—
                blew smoke into her mouth at night
& went to Mosgiel and Mitre 10 twice

She wears additional eyelashes
& cannot say thank you easily—

yet I tuck her in ~ pick her up ~ buy vegan treats

I see shoals pass over her—
see dawning—

yet she will ough blade me through—

become a head built by a stranger—
without fragrance—

bones oh a world—
jāā for glaciers

Blades (2015–2022)

each   new
cell   cell
is   next to bird song   is
new   each
now   now

Quartz concentration

each new cell is next to bird song

is new   each now

now

is shaped like a tide-scented plum

each

cell

our withhh of its whole

each

now

little edges bear rhythms

little rhythms at the edges

listen rain gather the red

centre the sound in your fall

hold the praise hold the praise

to the skin & seed of the galaxy

sapwood & land poetics

succulent in mouth

Pinch

The day a pinch / young /old / this now / your hand buffeting / heavy with air / speed / heat / along this now / not escaping / knowing this / but hovering / fleeting gaps / the breath between telegraph poles / leaning / sharp / buffeted / the window pressed to sky / to wheat / to some polaroid / this moment / this pinch / a time snag / an escape / not an escape / rushing in / rushing away / feeling the tether snap / swallowing the empty / onwards / because this is the road / throwing a shimmer of tongue / this moment now / this pinch / this short gasp / this no escape / this not empty / this sky-wheat / this red earth / this sped through / this growing / this harvest / this dissolving shell of sky / this ocean / this not mine

Notes

'Tender' is the sixth and conclusive iteration of a procedural poem in which each word beginning with T/t, E/e, N/n, D/d, E/e, R/r was replaced with 'Tender'/'tender' over six transpositions. The opening lines of 'Neck loss' are borrowed from a *Guardian* article by Oliver Milman ('Butterfly numbers plummeting in US west as climate crisis takes toll', 4 March 2021). 'Mishima confessions' translates and toys with a passage from *Confessions of a Mask* (1949, trans. 1958) by Yukio Mishima. The 'Kon Kon sequence' – the poems from 'fi / fi / fi / fi / fi / th / fi / fi / th / fi / to '♒   Aquarius   ♒' (but excluding 'Falling into water') – is based on a paragraph in an article by Candice Amich ('From precarity to planetarity: Cecilia Vicuña's *Kon Kon*', *The Global South* 7, 2013), and the absented ligatures (ff, fi, th, tt) that occurred in typographic transposition from a PDF to Word document. In the two full-page concrete poems (both titled 'ki') and 'Things fish say II', the use of 'ki' is adopted from Potawatomi botanist Robin Wall Kimmerer's suggestion to refer to non-human beings by the singular and plural pronouns 'ki' and 'kin' ('Nature needs a new pronoun: To stop the age of extinction, let's start by ditching "It"', *Yes Magazine*, 30 March 2015). 'Blessings on Joanna' converses with a poem ('Untitled', from *Imogen*, 1978, n.p.) and a painting (*The Plum Tree, Barry's Bay*, c. 1974–76) by Joanna Margaret Paul.

Acknowledgements

Ngā mihi nui and thank you to this small cottage on a narrow strip of land that merges indistinguishably with the whenua, trees and birds of Ōtepoti Dunedin's green belt. Most of the poems in *tung* were written in kōrero, in conversation, with this pulsing life.

Thank you to Te Whare Wānanga o Ōtākou the University of Otago for a PhD scholarship that supported me during the writing of these poems. Thank you in particular to the ākonga (students) and kaimahi (staff) of the English department, and especially my primary supervisor Jacob Edmond.

On the opposite side of the world, thank you to fellow residents, especially Essi Kausalainen, and staff at Saari Residence (Kone Foundation) in Mynämäki, Finland, with whom I shared a Finnish winter.

Back home, in this rohe, in this region, I would like to thank Emma Neale, Sue Wootton, Diane Brown, Carolyn McCurdie, Michelle Elvy, and other Otago poets and writers for their early support and invitations to read.

Special thanks to Rhian Gallagher for her time and generosity when I first started writing poetry in the immediate pre-Covid years, and to Alison Glenny for email and in-person poetry chats.

In the context of poetry competitions, I am grateful to David Eggleton, Vana Manasiadis and Vahni Capildeo for their insightful comments.

Arigatoo and thank you to friend and artist Motoko Kikkawa for chats and permission to use *Untitled* (2021) as the artwork for the cover.

A warm thank you to the editors and organisers of the following publications and institutions who first published or invited me to read versions of some of this work: *Landfall, Cordite, The Brotherton Poetry Prize Anthology* (London: Carcanet Press, 2020), *Fractured Ecologies* (Ålborg, Denmark: EyeCorner Press, 2020), *Kissing a Ghost: The New Zealand Poetry Society Anthology* (Wellington: The New Zealand Poetry Society, 2021), *Plumwood Mountain, amberflora*, Blue Oyster Art Project Space, Dunedin Public Art Gallery, New Zealand Young Writers Festival, NZ Poetry Shelf, *Otago Daily Times, Love in the Time of Covid, Antipodes: A Global Journal of Australian and New Zealand Literature, Southword* and *Stand Magazine*.

Final and heartfelt gratitude to Sue Wootton and the entire team at Otago University Press for publishing this, my first collection!

With love to my father always~

Published by Otago University Press
533 Castle Street
Dunedin, New Zealand
university.press@otago.ac.nz
www.oup.nz

First published 2023
Copyright © Robyn Maree Pickens
The moral rights of the author have been asserted

ISBN 978-1-99-004860-9

Editor: Anna Hodge
Cover: Motoko Kikkawa, *Untitled*, 2021, 420mm x 297mm, watercolour, collection of Anet Neutze and Scott Flanagan.

Printed in New Zealand by Ligare.